BLACK JACK
THE LUCKY CAT

WRITTEN BY
BERNADINE SEMINACK

Print information available on the last page

Rev. date: 12/16/2015

To order additional copies of this book, contact:
Xlibris
1-888-795-4274
www.Xlibris.com
Orders@Xlibris.com

Dedication:

To Cape May Animal Shelter &
Adoption Center's administration, staff
and volunteers who tirelessly provide
a professional and loving environment
for the animals in their care.

Mr. Brown moved way across town to be close to work Bob Brown had found.

Momma Miss and little Meg were fine but for Bob's son, Brandon, it was taking some time. He unpacked and aligned his toys on end but because of his move, he had no friends. Bob Brown thought of what to do because Brandon Brown was so sad, so blue. A pet he thought would save the day so off they went to the SPCA.

When Brandon went to pick a pet, he didn't know what to expect. The Shelter's doors both stout and wide kept all the animals safe inside. The noise he heard before he entered, alarmed him so he was unsettled.

Dogs bow wowing, snakes that slithered, cats meowing, a piggy wiggled, sheep that bleat and mice were in cages at his feet. A Cheshire cat grinned ear to ear but from the Siamese he sensed a sneer.

The dogs they wagged their happy tails but one Siberian just sat and wailed. A Great Dane stood a domineering stance but beneath his feet Chihuahuas danced. A Basset Hound's ear almost touched the floor but the Boxer's stare could not be ignored. An anxious dog, the Golden Retriever, would be quick to run just unlatch a lever. Brandon's eyes were wide with fright hoping the animals not sense his plight.

For choosing just one pet today, he'd have to keep the others at bay.

Brandon to a worker about to feed,

"Which pet here is a friend in need?"

"Black cats are averted because of their color so patrons usually choose another."

Just then Black Jack who'd outgrown his cage, put his paw on Brandon while the other's raged.

Now all the beasts sat at attention waiting to hear of Brandon's selection. It was a situation of little hope for those not chosen so up he spoke.

"All you pets are perfect picks I say but this one here has had a long stay. It's Black Jack, the cat, I say it's true though choosing him is so taboo. Because of his color adoption's unlikely but there's no truth to the fact black cats are unlucky. In Great Britain and Japan they are quite revered. Only in America are these cats feared."

15

So Brandon for Black Jack he paid his fee. And once and for all this feline was free. Before he packed his bag to go, he had to speak up and let others know.

"Listen up mates. Have no regrets. A new course has been set here for all you pets. From this day on," Brandon wrote, "no longer will you be judged by just your coat."

Hoorays were heard in every cage. Alas for this feline his luck had changed

And here we are at the happy end. Black Jack and Brandon had both found friends.

Printed in the United States
By Bookmasters